TROTTER 2020: A SOUTHERN BLACK MAN'S VIEW

By: Jimmie Trotter

1

Published by

PUBLISHING

Jodi Lynn

EDITING

Jodi Lynn SB Publishing and Editing, Pensacola, FL 32526
abasilence@gmail.com Phone: (931) 591-5300

ISBN-13: 979-8-64-055526-4

LIBRARY OF CONGRESS #: 2020907952

Printed in the United States

Cover Image: J. Trotter Photography

Dedication

I'd like to dedicate this book to two of my colleagues that are brothers that are ironically running against each other in the current County Commissioner's race, Lumon and LuTimothy May. I have had conversations with both, and somewhat understand, and admire their individual pursuits of excellence and leadership that causes them to run in the same race. Thank you, for being leaders and trailblazers in our community.

Also, I'd like to salute my church, Jubilee International Ministry and our Pastor, Len Ballenger. A church that truly looks like heaven with its rainbow color of ethnicities all worshiping and uniting in a multicultural praise to God.

I must honor my friends, Pete and Cheryl Foster. With this dedication, I attempt to immortalize them as two people who have eyes that can see beyond a color difference, and hands that are always open to give and help. They have befriended and supported me, and have been my help from the sanctuary.

And, most of all, I'd like to dedicate this book to my wife, Cathy Friesen Trotter, who moved some 3000 miles from her hometown in British Colombia, Canada, to take a chance on love with a guy that she met on the internet. Her smile always mesmerizes me, and her laughter is contagious. Thank you, Cathy, for always giving me your heart.

Table of Contents

Reviews

"Moving to the South, I have experience a completely different way of life. I've told my husband, and many others, that my first year of marriage was my happiest, and most heartbreaking, all wrapped up in one. I learned a lot that year about life as an interracial couple, what it was like to grow up in the South, as well as, how black and white people interacted.

In this book, Jimmie will take you on his journey through life in the Deep South. I promise you won't be disappointed, and it may actually leave you craving more…"

- *Mrs. Cathy Trotter*

"Having grown up in the North, I have often wondered what it was like for those who are Southern natives. Where every day I wake up and thank God that I now live in Florida, do the natives feel the same way about living in this part of the world? While I love it in the South, I still couldn't help but to think that there is something more to be revealed, something hidden to be searched out. What was/is it like being a native Southerner?

TROTTER 2020: A SOUTHERN BLACK MAN'S VIEW *answered questions that I've wondered about as I've embraced my new life in the South, and began experiencing the good ole Southern hospitality. The door is opened, and we have been invited to take a seat at the table to hear "the Southern Black Man's" point of view on then, and now. Prepare to be captivated, from beginning to end."*

- *Jodi L. Serino-Barbour, Self-Published Author*
Entrepreneur

TROTTER 2020:

A SOUTHERN

BLACK MAN'S

VIEW

By: Jimmie Trotter

Introduction

I'd like to say, my writings are an effort in posterity to take words and actions that we've heard, seen, and evidenced in an attempt to etch them into your memory; and, even more so, into history. I understand that some may feel that it has a racial undertone, which is unfortunate because that is not my aim. My subject matter comes from firsthand experiences and accounts; so, again, if I offend you, it may be that you simply misunderstood my intent.

I am writing this book in a time when our world and nation are struggling with a virus that's been deemed a "Pandemic". Covid-19 has been sweeping across the world, and is now in our nation. This virus is taking its toll in the Black community. In many of our neighborhoods, and our communities, we are often unable to practice the recommended social distancing promoted by health officials.

The current data is showing that we have to take heed to the warnings about this contagion. Along with the staggering number of new cases of infection, in the black community, the government - both locally and nationally, will need to step up their aid to these crippled areas. This is the time when leaders, and champions, rise up to make their voices heard, and their faces seen.

My hope is that I will remind you that we are a nation of champions who only know victory because we built our nation on a victorious God who can't be defeated. We stand in the midst of this fight knowing that there is no weapon, and no virus, formed against this great nation that will prosper. So, I welcome you to venture with me as we walk this walk of champions

in a nation of champions.

Remind You

Let me remind you of what is true,
the fearfully made and awesome you.
Maybe God colored your skin to remind you.

Where others give up and go home,
you must continue, and work alone;
Your will always relentless and strong

Maybe God colored your skin to remind you
of all the wonders that He has for you;
of all the feats that He would do through you.

So, straighten the shoulders and walk tall
for the task at hand is your high call.
He is with you, and won't let you fall.

And, at the end of time, your reward will be due
for the fight that you have been through;
a crown of life just to remind you.

J. Trotter

Chapter 1: So That We All Know My Neighborhood

I listened to my grandparents, and their peers, refer to each other with prefixes of Mr. Johnny, and Ms., or Mrs. Mary. I thought, *"How strange."* I later understood that, in their earlier years of struggling through racism and slavery, these people had never received respect from their owners, or society, here in America; and, they may have even felt that they never would.

However, they enforced, and insulated, their dignity by respecting themselves. "Mr." Johnny got a sense of being a man by hearing his friends, and neighbors, use that simple prefix in their salutations despite his second-grade education, and lack of job skills, other than being a servant. Old "Mrs." Mary knew that her dignity and worth, as a lady, had long been stolen away; but, that prefix somehow restored her innocence. In every greeting, I saw and heard what they didn't have to say. I knew I was in the company of a people of courage, a people of strength, a people of dignity; and I write this so that we all know.

Hold My Hand

Take a deep breath, and smell it.
It's the wind of change, embrace it.

The thing that once held you down,
Becoming your glory, and your crown;

The situation, that always was your defeat,
Is shifting to become solid ground for your feet

Where they once wouldn't let you in,
The door swings wide open on the hinge.

But, it's still too early to celebrate
Although the progress we've made is no mistake.

Because I still need you to hold my hand
Until it is recorded, in history, my friend

That a man's worth is not determined by the color of
his skin

J. Trotter

Chapter 2: Checklist

There are some basic fundamentals that were commonly found in solid Black family units. First, and foremost, there would be a solid God-grounded foundation, which included regular church attendance by everyone in the household. In the Black community, there was a time where church attendance was never an issue. It was common knowledge that "everyone" attended church. Whenever mom and dad went to church, all the kids went also. It was never left to the kids, and teenagers, to decide whether they would attend, or not. Attendance was mandatory.

Secondly, your behavior in the Black community was indicative of your church going. You were expected to act like a God-honoring, and fearing, family. Parents would instruct their kids at home about proper and improper behavior, with consequences, if necessary. In our hearts was the knowledge that, no matter what the next minute of life would bring, as long as we had God in the minute before, we could endure.

God was our safe place. We could run into His presence and find refuge. Refuge from what? From everything that daily living in a racially divided life in the South could bring. In our songs, and hymns, we could escape our anger, our shame, and our abuse; and find a strength that can only come from believing in God, that He was not far removed from us, but present. He was more present, and necessary, than even our next breath. Believing that God was, without a doubt, for us, meant that it didn't matter who was against us.

Heroes

Little Black boys playing in the Southern streets,
No worries, no concerns just summer heat.

Back at home, Daddy's gone.
These boys have to learn to be men on their own.

Looking for heroes to emulate,
Dreams of success, thoughts of being great.

In the back of their minds, the search continues
without end;
Looking for how to be strong Black men.

When they look at you what will they find,
to give them hope in their little minds?
Because, my friend, the only true heroes they will see
are the everyday ones that are in you and me.

J. Trotter

Chapter 3: Heroes

In every black community, there were heroes. In my little town of Lillian, Alabama, there was a man whom we shall call Charlie S. Charlie signed his name with an "X"; and with little to no education, he ran a septic business. This man, without the ability to read, or write, singlehandedly acquired the reputation of being the go-to guy in the industry. People countywide would run this man down for his services.

I remember being in a lineup of cars trailing behind his huge truck, in tow with a septic tank, or large excavator, traveling at some 40 or 45 miles per hour, on 55 mile per hour highways. I doubt that he owned a driver's license; but, no matter, all the local policemen knew, and admired, this man. Now, I want you to understand that Charlie, with his business, had also become the richest man in our neighborhood. His brick home, of probably some 3000, or so, square feet, and large shed, complete with a gas pump to fuel his equipment, were evidence of that fact.

But, the greatest hero of them all was my granddad, Johnny Trotter. With only a second grade education, my granddad would often struggle through commentaries, and his bible, in order to superintend and teach class in Sunday school at church. I remember there were nights when he would come to me and ask me to help him enunciate, and explain, words that, as a junior high school kid, I could help him understand. Johnny would take his hunting dog, or his cast net, and leave the house, and come back with dinner for our grandma to prepare for the kids and grandkids. Then, there were those snack cakes. I never will forget the "day old" snack cakes that he would get from one of his landscaping clients from the Sunbeam bread store. My brothers and I would warm those snack cakes on a wood burning heater; and, along with all the neighborhood kids, eat them as breakfast before we would jump in line to catch our school bus. It's interesting how those snack cakes, given by a couple of white people brought such a sense of well-being and joy to an entire neighborhood of poor black kids.

Now my grandma, Mary Trotter, on the other hand, was a bit of a disciplinarian. She would tell me, *"When you come in from school, you do your chores and you do your homework; and if there is time before dark, you play with your friends, and if not, oh well."* It was made clear that I would get my "learning" first, and girlfriends, and other activities would come later.

She was tough, but always fair. She helped me get my priorities straight. She made sure that I got the basics. Would there be value in the Black community if we go back to instilling the basics that we once learned? We need to tell our kids that they have to do their chores, and their homework, before they can play their video games. Maybe we should instill that education comes first, and "booty calls" later. Well, parents and grandparents, it is up to you. Make sure they do their homework.

Lost And Found

Years ago, I lost my self-respect.
Today, as I was respecting you, I found it.

I can't remember when it was, but I lost my dignity.
As I worked with the elderly, they gave it back to me.

I had lost the value of our country's liberty.
My visits with prisoners in jail gave it back to me.

I had even lost the joy of living and giving,
until the eyes of my grandbaby showed me what I was
missing.

Now, I know the awe of life in every sight and sound,
because I no longer live life in the lost and found.

J. Trotter

Chapter 4: The Right Thang

Going through my teenage years there were always opportunities to get into trouble. This is the time of life when kids need strong parents that will diligently steer them in the right direction. Fortunately, I had that in my grandparents. Also, along that time, Afro-American film maker and producer, Spike Lee, came along with a movie that depicted difficult situations in the lives of Blacks in a comical setting.

As these various difficult situations escalated, to the point of necessary resolution, the underlying theme was to "Do The Right Thing", which was also the title of the movie, such a simple way at looking at life; but also, so profound. So, while you are out doing life today, and that co-worker, or store clerk, or significant other, or in-law, or client starts to work your nerves, before you respond ... take a deep breath, and "Do the Right Thang".

The "right thang" could often get twisted, (meaning confused, or distorted.) For example, I was talking with a young Black man whose childhood years had been abusive and rough. Although, there had been a male figure in his life during those years, there had been no real nurturing or bonding. He confessed to me that he was having a hard time securing a job. But, then, he also explained that when Christmas and special occasions would come around, he wouldn't have money for gifts.

His solution to his problem, he said, was that he would steal gifts and things for his girlfriend, so that she would have nice stuff. I got the impression that he viewed this as an act of true love, or chivalry. I was really at a loss but wondered if as a race, have our

values and need for love, or acceptance, fallen so low?

Has the greatest country in the world reduced our self-

worth to the acquisition of stuff as our measuring

stick? Has our youth become a society of avarice

monsters? All I know that our love for our significant

others, and people who we adore, can't find its

fulfillment in conduct like this.

Always There

They are always there,
Good times and bad,
Always showing they care.

Old ones are so dear,
Although they may be far,
They are always near.

New ones take time to find,
But they will come to you.
Just be kind.

Without them a pauper you will be.
For priceless is the value
Of true friends, you see.

J. Trotter

Chapter 5: So That We All Know

To get to know Trotter 2020, I have to take you back to Trotter 1970. As a third grader, the new federal mandate to integrate took our school bus to a previously "all white" school - Elberta Junior High School in Elberta, Alabama. Elberta was a little southern town with a strong German heritage. This little town wouldn't allow any Walmarts, or McDonalds, or any large stores of any type within their community; and they definitely were not in favor of having black kids invade their schools.

As our bus pulled to a halt, and we stepped into the quad, white students were standing on both sides of the walkway. They had a harmonious chant: *"Nigger, nigger!"* This led to inevitable fighting behind the gymnasium for the entire first year of school. But, in the midst of all this madness, I encountered the wisdom of an underpaid white principal, Mr. B. After all the fighting that integration brought onto the newly integrated school grounds, in the south, in the late 60's, things did calm down with only an occasional quarrel here and there. These individual spats were usually followed by a trip to the principal's office resulting in paddling and/or suspension. On one of my trips to the office after a conflict, my entire outlook on school and human interaction took an unexpected shift. The principal, Mr. B, sat me down and said, *"Jimmie you are a smart kid. Cats and dogs fight. People can reason and talk about their differences."*

Little did this middle aged, skinny, southern white man of some meager 140lbs know; but, he had just rocked the world of a scared, and twisted, little 10-year-old black kid. He swept away all the aggression and anger that I had in me. He pointed and shot me into my future, like an arrow without any prejudice, or bias, toward any man; because, after all, we were not cats or dogs, and we could reason and talk out any differences.

Tip your hats Alabama, Florida, Mississippi, Georgia, Tennessee, and all of America to the wisdom of Mr. B. This wisdom moved me, and pushed me, to find a way to communicate. No longer was I this guy who voiced his pain and aggression by punching and kicking. I was now on a mission to pursue a better way, a verbal way, to conflict resolution.

Mirror, mirror I know you recall
All the pain and strain, you remember it all.

But, it has only made me strong.
I've learned to do right when done wrong.

Mirror, mirror you've become my friend
for in you I see the reflection of God's hand.

Mirror, mirror always call me back
so I can see the fact,

That God has created a masterpiece in me
for all the world to see.

His vessel strong, secure, and true;
so when the world looks, Lord, you will get the honor
and praise due.

J. Trotter

Chapter 6: My brother's keeper

In the following years, in junior high, I excelled in class and enjoyed being a leader in track, field, and basketball. The kids, that were at one time considered enemies, were now friends and colleagues. It may seem menial, and maybe even uncomfortable; but, the next time you talk with a person of a different race, or culture, look them directly in the eye. Go ahead! I dare you to make an effort to get unquestionable eye contact. Look them right in the eye.

When I make this conscious effort with people, without fail, I gain the ability to really "see" them, and engage with them. It's like you see the other person's humanity. You can see their frailty. You actually look into their soul, and see their present emotional state. But, be warned; once you do this act you will have crossed the line; and now, you will become vulnerable to your own feelings. Your feelings of an obligation to connect with, comfort, and console a fellow human being.

There is a God-given switch inside of you that automatically switches on when you look another person right in the eye. You see beyond their flesh and into their soul; and it tugs at the God-nature inside of you. It makes you know that, beyond the shadow of a doubt, we all are really connected. So, go ahead, look right into your neighbor's eyes; and, deep inside, you will behold your brother's keeper.

The Connection

I guess you instantly saw the look in my eyes,

It showed all the questions, what ifs, and whys.

The obvious difference I could clearly see;

but somehow they all attracted, and lured me.

You called it refreshing,

I called it reviving.

The difference between you and me,

But the connection was obvious for all to see.

The connection that made us a match

was the same connection that infuriated some, in fact.

You see, the difference was the color of our skin.

We had crossed the line drawn in the sand by men.

Scandalous, some even called it a sin;

But, if we had to, we would do it all again.

Because the only wrong I could find, my friend,

Was the hatred that resided deep in the hearts of men.

J. Trotter

Chapter 7: The Difference

In the South, the races have lived as enemies for so long that it is a bit uncomfortable to watch our kids grow up playing and doing life together. Of course, the natural progression of all this familiarity leads to dating; and in some cases, marriage. My wife and I are in an interracial marriage; and I believe that I, subconsciously, keep my eyes peeled for other interracial relationships when I am out and about. It seems, as if, I see more couples that have embraced the difference in cultures, and moved into committed relationships.

I, also, still notice some of the stares that are given by people who don't approve of the mixing of races. These stares make it apparent that the hearts of many people, here in the Deep South, are still poisoned by their racist heritage. I would have you to know that this staring comes from people of both the Black and White community. I guess I would like to go on record here and encourage, and salute, all the couples who have decided, and are deciding, to commit to an interracial relationship. You are shaping our little world, as we know it, here in the Deep South.

I'd like to emphasize the point that these relationships are built, and solidified, on the differences that the couples find in each other. In other words, they celebrate the uniqueness that they find in the culture of their mates. It's the "opposites attract" effect with a splash of cultural diversity. Sure, their mate is a different color or ethnicity; and, perhaps, sees things from a different viewpoint; but, that's the point.

That ability to see from a different viewpoint allows for a broader perspective of any, and every subject, or idea. So, here's the deal; when presented with a problem or idea, an interracial couple has the advantage of seeing the problem from two totally different angles, from the "heads", and the "tails", side of the issue. This brings a unique flavor to problem solving that may be otherwise missed. Viva la difference!!!

Don't forget to be kind to your brother.
Don't forget to love him.

Don't forget to always have his best interest at heart.
Don't forget to lift him up in prayer.

Don't forget that, in all his dreams and aspirations,
don't forget to play your part.

Don't forget that we are all part of this big blended
family.
Don't forget that's why we need this brotherly creed.

For God watches and make us give an account of every
deed.

Don't forget.

J. Trotter

Chapter 8: Leave your Shoes at the Door

In some cultures, taking off your shoes, when entering a friend's home, is expected. Whereas, here in the Deep South, wiping your feet, at the door, on a door mat is more than enough. I've also found, and maybe you have noticed this, that some of the people that we associate with, on odd occasions, are not so keen on inviting minorities into their home. Barring the fact that you might be hired on as a maid, or performing some odd job inside the house, you don't come beyond the doorway.

Okay, I can understand this type of thinking if you are in a high crime district or if you are dealing with a complete stranger; but, I am talking about nearby neighbors and colleagues at work. I must say that I've also seen the reverse and known minorities that don't allow their Caucasian associates to breach the perimeter of their doorway. It may be here that we have the root of the issue. Maybe we have seen ourselves as enemies for so long that we have fortified ourselves in our homes, and drawn a line that won't allow the enemy into our camp. Come on, go ahead, next time and invite them in. Who knows, they may even leave their shoes at the door.

When You Know Who You Are

When you know who you are,
you won't need to exploit your brother's differences.

When you know who are,
your words will reflect an inner love for all men.

When you know who you are,
you will see your strength as an answer to your
brother's weakness.

When you know who you are,
Working alongside your brother will be a joy, and a
lesson in unity.

When you know who you are,
you will walk with men of all nations and cultures;
And you will call them all your brothers
when you know who you are.

J. Trotter

Chapter 9: Like Heaven

Here in the South, we still have churches that are all white, or all black. I saw a church for Koreans the other day. Okay, I am thinking, *"OH, come on."* Help me, but does anyone really think that when they get to heaven that they will tell Jesus that they want to attend the all-white church, or all-black church, or all Korean church around the corner? *"I THINK NOT!!!"*

My thinking is that heaven is going to be a mixture of all types, and colors, of people living in the presence of God. Shouldn't we 'get to practicing' that type of church right now, here on earth? I mean doesn't that make sense? I would go as far as advising you to go looking for a church that looks like the population of heaven. It may be just my thinking, but your church home should look like heaven shouldn't it?

The Talk

You know what they say about you.
You wonder if they even know what's true.
In your mind, it's like everyone doubts you.
They doubt your sincerity, your motives, what will you
do?

You have to find a way to respond,
Before all your hope is gone.
It's like you are fighting this battle all alone.
You don't know if you can carry on.

But, then you remember when
You heeded the voice of a friend
That told you that when these battles begin
You can always win.

Because it's your conversation within
That determines your end,
It's the way you talk to yourself
That silences the voice of everyone else.

So be diligent, and always true
To take the time to talk to you.

J. Trotter

Chapter 10: The Key

Seeing all the struggle going on in our neighborhoods, and in the nation, in general, self-talk has been a way of survival. I believe it was a poem by Walter D. Wintle that says it all, *".... But sooner or later the man who wins is the one who thinks he can."* The voice that is inside of you can give you confidence. The voice that is inside of you can also bring the champion in you to the battlefield. Oh, and believe me, the battle is real. Every day, every hour, every minute, every second the battle rages in our mind and in the world. So, I live on a diet of steady self-talk, affirming myself, and my actions.

As kids, we all grow up wanting to be accepted. All of us, needing to be approved. One of my earliest memories of my youth, as a 4 or 5-year-old, has always been a vision of me playing with a toy dump truck in our sandy front yard in Lillian, Alabama; alone, no neighboring kids, or friends around – just me, alone and content. As adults, we all see, and yearn for, that contentment that we see in the eyes and faces of kids. Before you can become a champion, you have to find the path of access to that peace and contentment.

Without this peace, you won't be able to master your emotions when difficult situations come up. Without this peace, there will be no joy in your family time. Without this peace, the conversations with your significant others will lack connection. This peace will allow you to cope with situations that you can't change, and tolerate the flaws inherit in everyday people. You see, success patiently waits to reward you and me when we use our self-talk as the key. The path of access to this peace can only be found in quiet time.

This quiet time has to be intentional – a scheduled time

where you are alone; a time when there are no

distractions. This is the time when a champion is

created; when he can hear the voice of his creator. The

only way to peace is to go inside and hear that part of

you that knows the maker of the universe.

Every champion knows the value of this intimate

time. The champion knows that without this intimate

connection everything is lost. Without this intimacy

everything is nothing. Without this intimacy every

battle is already fought and lost. This connection is the

champion's vital necessity. It is more vital than the air

he breathes. The champion would rather die a thousand

deaths rather than live a single moment without this

connection. Show me the layman who knows this

intimacy, and you will reveal a champion.

The New You

The times are changing.
They are changing just for you.
It's time to reinvent yourself,
just like brand new.

It's time to learn more, to be more.
There is nothing stopping you.
The sky is the limit.
It's all on you.

You are in the land of plenty.
The opportunities are so many.
The decision is up to you.
What do you want to do?

It's not about color, or race.
You are the one setting your pace.
So forget the shame.
There is no one to blame.
Show us the "New You"

J. Trotter

Chapter 11: Maturity

I know that no one likes hard times; but, have you noticed that in hard times you have to dig deep inside and find that inner strength to fight through the situation? Let's face it, when things are going well, we rarely learn anything. We kind of go on autopilot and cruise through our days almost oblivious to everything. In hard times, we learn lessons from life. We often learn lessons that make us stronger, and prepare us for new things, and opportunities that come along in the future.

Let's face it, some of those hard times will come at you, and knock you off your feet; and that's okay, because being knocked down doesn't mean you are knocked out. However, while you are regaining your composure, I want to give you a little nugget that could be a game changer for you; establish your footing by investing in someone else. There you go. You read it right. You heard it in your head. Leverage your success, and shift the momentum of the situation by investing in someone else. Look around you, in your neighborhood, or at work, or at church. Find that lonely elderly person, that brother, or sister in a struggle, that disconnected teenager. Become that breath of fresh air, and Godsend that can bring relief to their situation. You can be that elixir that brings healing, a made to order home remedy.

Add just one more ingredient into your recipe. Most people are gracious, kind, and grateful when things are good; but, the trick is, can you be grateful when things are not going your way? Can you be grateful when the pipe at the water heater springs a leak and floods the house with an inch or so of water? Can you be grateful when you show up at your arrival point at the airport, but your luggage doesn't? How about when your kids, who are out of your home, and starting their own families, are ungrateful although you are going out of your way, and spending your time and money to help them with their problems; and they even have the nerve to cop an attitude with you? Okay, so be grateful. It shows your level of maturity.

I Forgot

I forgot to hug my kids today
I just sent them out and, on their way.

I forgot to call that significant other on the phone.
Well, it's okay. They probably weren't at home.

I forgot to laugh with my friends;
but, it's okay, I'm sure we will all get together later
again.

I forgot to appreciate my parents,
and apologize for them having to pay all those months
of rents.

I forgot to thank all the people that teach me so much
about life, and how to live, and such.

All these people had enriched my life with their birth.
Then, I woke up, and they were in heaven while I was
missing them here on earth.

J. Trotter

Chapter 12: Perspective

As we look at, and deal with, inequality and discrimination, you have to know who you are. Know that you are fearfully and wonderfully made. Know that you are unique and one of a kind, causing you to be rare and valuable. There is always value in rareness. There is no one in the universe with the same smile and laugh as you. You are a success just looking for a place to happen. And more than all this, know whose you are. You are a child of the king, the Highest God, the ruler of heaven and earth. His favor surrounds you like a shield, and you are the apple of his eye. He is for you, and no foe can stand against you.

With this knowledge, and self-image, you can now change the "perspective" that others might have of you and your culture by offering new information. The

Specialist calls it a "paradigm shift". For example, your appreciation of a stranger might change once he, or she, discloses that they are a military vet. I have seen this shift as I interact with people of different cultures and I often wonder if it is just that simple. If I could, by simply changing your environment for a short period of time, through a person you met, or a book you read, or perhaps something you listened to or watched, change your perspective? I have come to believe that it is actually that simple. Now that you are aware of the simplicity of this process of "paradigm shift", I think you realize that you are in debt to society, in debt to the Deep South, to give them information that will help them with their perspective on racism. Who knows? You could cause a paradigm shift. Who knows?

The Code

It doesn't need to be said, you know it;

you've got to work harder,

you've got to be smarter.

You may get paid less;

but, you have to be the best.

They may never ask you the question;

but, you have to know the answers, every one.

You get your application in first,

although you get considered last.

And make sure your smile is bigger, and brighter;

because you are not going to be denied simply because

of your color.

J. Trotter

Chapter 13: Winning

I believe we all have the desire to do well and pursue success to one degree or another. Without ambition, or a dream, we would have no true reason to continue on in life. That dream, or ambition, is depicted in the single mom striving to provide for her kids; or the businessman pressing to secure clientele to keep his employees on staff. As I look into the faces of inmates, during visits at various local jail facilities, I can easily say that goal attainment has a more relevant consequence of changing who you become, as you move towards your goals. If you reach your goals, but you don't become a person of values; if you reach your goals, but you don't like the person that stares back at you from the mirror; if you reach your goals, but your attitude is always jacked-up; if you reach your goals, and you have not become a bigger and better person, then you lose. So, take note of all the consequences that are relevant as you strive for your goals so that you, in the end, really win.

As we are growing, and reaching goals, it is easy to hold on to past and present injustice that we suffer as a Black culture. We can't live in the anger and anxiety that suffered wrongs might bring. So, how do we cope? How do we live beyond the madness? We have to start each day with a clean slate. Each day is a new day that God has given us. We don't live in the past or dread the future. We live in the "present" - the present, the gift of a new day. So, come with me, and let's enjoy this gift, and start it with a clean slate. Start your day with a clean slate, and expect something good to happen today.

Here is a key to having a good day: Always plant a seed in advance. That's the key. If you want a good day today, plant a good seed yesterday. If you want apples in your orchard today, you must plant seeds for that tree in advance. In addition, if you are planting grape seeds, don't expect apple trees. Here's the deal, if you have been walking around complaining, moaning, and groaning about your life, do you really expect positive, motivating, and progressive things to happen? There is an ebb and flow in life, a unique balance. You have to recognize that this balance is going to primarily give back to you what you put in. Come on, let's work the system. Live your life in "the balance".

The Same

Society said we were not the same,
Different hair, different color, and different name.

The places we came from were not the same,
Different culture, different people, and different game.

Our parent's views were not the same,
Different rules, different rituals, who is to blame?

Then, one day, everything changed.
Water fountains, voting rights and schools all became
the same.

Now, we see all the thoughts about difference were
insane;
because we really are all quite... the same.

J. Trotter

Chapter 14: Check-Up

I have a quiz for you. Don't get nervous. But here it goes… I was just recalling a conversation I had with a friend of mine. She was conveying to me how her family had pretty much "dis-owned" her because they disapproved of her being a white female in a relationship with a black male. Now I have all these thoughts spinning in my head. Am I sadder for her or for her parents? Am I just mad at her parents for their pompous attitude? Should I have expected this type of arrogance here in the Deep South?

So, here's the quiz: If your little sweet Susie came home for the holidays, and low and behold, *"guess who's coming to dinner?"* Or, your Johnny calls, and says that he has decided to get married to this woman; and you didn't even know that he was in an interracial relationship. Would you pass the test? Would you be concerned about how people would view all of you together as a family? I mean what would your friends say, and think? Could they come to church with you? Would they feel welcomed? Could they move into your neighborhood? And what if they decided to have kids?

Well, there it is ladies and gentlemen, parents, and grandparents, there is your litmus test. Do the test. Oh, and no cheating....

Who Could Have Known?

Who could have known the power housed in man
when they work together hand in hand.

A cohesive unified effort
All empowered through, and by it.

Who could have known
this power that we have honed?

By dropping the lies that once deceived,
and all the judgments preconceived;

But, now we know the truth,
and proudly display it before our youth.

And who could have known
that this would truly set them free;
so, that they could live beyond racial tyranny.

J. Trotter

Chapter 15: New Life

Today, I want you to imagine myself and all your friends, and family, pulling you into a meeting. We are all together for an intervention on your behalf; however, this intervention is a little bit different. It is an intervention for your re-invention. In the business world, when your profit margin starts to dwindle, and your target market, of buyers, are beginning to buy from your competition, you re-invent your product, or service. Today, we are going to re-invent you.

There are a couple of things that concern us; and we feel that we need to bring them to your attention because we love you. We have noticed that you don't smile as much as you ought to. We love your smile; it brightens the room, and it makes everyone around you feel appreciated. We know that you have to deal with the media image that depicts you in a negative way; but, we believe that your smile will instantly clear up that misconception.

Also, we haven't heard your laughter in months. Laughter is medicine for the soul you know. Our souls are sickened from a lack of hearing your laughter; so, we know that your soul must be dying for the nourishment that your laughter gives. Your laughter will kill all the lies and accusations of your haters. Finally, we need you to look at us. There is a look in your eyes that always gives us hope; a hope that believes for tomorrow; a hope that believes for the best. Without that look of hope, we will give up. We are your family. We need you, and we hope that you will do your re-invention.

The Times

Just as fashions come
and fashions go;

Just as the seas must ebb
and then flow;

Men's prejudice will wither
with the wind of time we know,

And then with this change
Society will grow.

So let those winds come,
and let them blow;

Because our history needs to know
the healing that only time can show.

J. Trotter

Chapter 16: Your Enemy

Let's make up a scenario: In this scenario, we have a known enemy. This enemy despises us for no valid reason; but, the hatred is real. Now, the knowledge of this enemy, will in itself, attempt to generate a mindset toward your oppressor. I must warn you that this knowledge has the potential to turn you into something sinister. This knowledge has the power to transform you into an inhumane terror, a true menace to society.

So, I feel that we must form a strategy that will insulate you from this demon inherent in your knowledge. Here is what I found we must do: We will deal with this enemy on the physical plane, because we will interact with him daily in our society. In addition, we will draw on the wisdom of an ancient teacher that found himself, and His people, in the same dilemma. We will engage this enemy on a spiritual plane – the plane where his deep hatred is harbored; the plane where mindsets and knowledge collide. We will pray for our enemies. We will pray for our haters. Now, be advised, this teacher knew that, as you engaged your enemy, in spiritual assault, your attack would not only neutralize your foe, but it would turn your fight against them into a fight for them. So, now I need you to look into the eyes of your enemy, and tell me, *"WHOSE SIDE ARE YOU ON?"*

Reconciled

Somehow, can you redeem the time?
Time lost loving them;
your neighbors, your friends, your kids, your kin

So wrapped up...
In hatred,
in color,
in yourself.

Maybe you just need to humble yourself;
Ask for forgiveness from God, and everyone else.
Start over again, just like new,
See things from their point of view.

Then, something wonderful can happen,
Not inside them; but, rather, in you.tt
It's the power of reconciliation.
It's waiting for you.

J. Trotter

Chapter 17: Are We Ready?

The South has always set the racial climate of our nation. Occasionally, you will have a Rodney King incident or something of that sort in the North. But, if you want to know what the racial condition of the United States is, you have to go where all the battles for freedom were fought – here in the South.

Currently, I am a candidate for County Commissioner in the State of Florida. The Office of County Commissioner is a fairly high-ranking local office. It carries some political weight in local government. I expect this venture will put a demand on the racial atmosphere here in Pensacola. It will challenge the mindset of the majority white demographic, in my district, to examine their position on equality.

There are five members on the Board of Commissioners; one representing each of the five districts in Escambia County. In our county, we have one district that is designated a majority-minority district; meaning that the majority of the residents, in this district, are people of color. It is designed to ensure that people of color will have a representative on the board of commissioners. The district geographical lines are moved from time to time, supported by census data, to ensure that this majority-minority ratio stays in place. Sounds admirable, right?

It would seem that this is a step, in the right direction, for equality and inclusion. However, the downside of this is that, moving these district lines, as our population and demographics change, ensures that you will always have one, and only one, (almost never a second, or third) person of color on the Board of Commissioners, at any time, because you have made the dominant demographic group a majority in all other districts. Unfortunately, this ensures that your minority population remains a minority in representation.

Current demographics show, at the printing of this book, that nearly 40% of Escambia County is of minority status. This data means that the Board of Commissioners would need to have not one, but two, of their five seats occupied by people of color in order to properly represent the population of this area. This is a change that has to be both identified and resolved in our local government. This is the current change that needs to be made regardless of the resistance that the community might have so that a federal mandate will not be necessary.

I am running in a district that is not the majority-minority district, which creates a scenario that allows us to subtly check the mindset of our southern community. Has our community grown to a level of maturity and change that will look beyond skin color and cultural bias? Inclusively, in my race, all the candidates have basically the same platform that includes infrastructure changes, more communication with the community, and the like. So, the primary question would be, is this district, comprised of some 44,000 registered voters, ready to add more color to the current administration? They have voiced that they want change; but, are they ready for change that might include a person of color?

Let me add here that I was talking to a client the other day, who happens to be Caucasian, and just out of the blue she mentioned something to me. She stated that she is an entrepreneur that moved here from the North; and that, she frequently gets ousted on business deals for this reason. It seems that conversations with prospective clients will be going well until they are informed that she is from "north of the Mason-Dixon" – a line that divided the northern and southern (free and slave, respectively) states in the 1800's, in the American Civil War era. So here it is… her training, Master's degree, experience, and referrals are all of no value to her because she was not born in the Deep South.

Are we, as a community, ready for inclusion; ready to get rid of the "good ole boy" mentality, and move forward, so that our nation can move forward? Again, remember as the South goes, so goes our nation's racial climate. As a godly man, I wonder if our churches are ready to no longer allow 'the Sunday church hour' to be the most racially divided hour of the week. I wonder if the church is ready to come out of the silent majority, and take its place in the political arena, by grooming candidates, and putting them in office by voting.

Will the church awaken to its God-given mandate to rule, and reign, in governmental arenas? If we could only awaken, and activate, this sleeping giant called the church, we could have righteousness in high places, in local and national government. We have proclaimed ourselves to be one nation under God, and that being said, we must have godly leaders. Are we

ready?

THANKS!

I would just like to say, to all my friends and readers, that as I give these accounts they are not relayed with a grudge, or a chip, on my shoulder. In fact, I would like to thank all the people of different backgrounds and various races that encourage and embrace this forum. It's the simple, everyday common things that all of you do that show that our climate here in the South, and in America, is changing. Thank you for the simple things, like a casual conversation in a grocery store line, the simple gesture of holding the door, as an act of kindness, or an early morning salutation in passing. Those simple things that say, we are all human, so let's do this together. So, thanks again, for helping change the world as we know it.

About The Author

Self-published Author Jimmie Trotter digs holes, and installs sod, as a successful landscaper and sprinkler installer in beautiful Pensacola, Florida. Being raised by his grandparents, only minutes across the Alabama border in Lillian, Jimmie has experienced southern living all of his life.

Jimmie walks into the halls of the work release, and mandated rehab facilities, that he has ministered in for the past 15 years, and often says, *"if all the people in your circle are of the same color and culture as you*

are, then your circle is too small!"

Jimmie, and his Canadian wife, Cathy, minister together in both the jails and their non-denominational church, Jubilee International Ministries. It can be said that their interracial marriage is a ministry of reconciliation of the races.

Made in the USA
Monee, IL
09 May 2020